The Severson Sisters Super Girl Guide To

RESPECT

The Severson Sisters
Super Girl Guide To

RESPECT

The Severson Sisters

NEW YORK

The Severson Sisters Super Girl Guide To

RESPECT

ISBN 978-1-61448-425-7 paperback
ISBN 978-1-61448-426-4 eBook
Library of Congress Control Number: 2012949653

Morgan James Publishing
The Entrepreneurial Publisher
5 Penn Plaza, 23rd Floor,
New York City, New York 10001
(212) 655-5470 office • (516) 908-4496 fax
www.MorganJamesPublishing.com

Cover Design by:
Brenda Haun
BHaundesigns@gmail.com

Interior Design by:
Bonnie Bushman
bonnie@caboodlegraphics.com

In an effort to support local communities, raise awareness and funds, Morgan James Publishing donates a percentage of all book sales for the life of each book to Habitat for Humanity Peninsula and Greater Williamsburg.

Get involved today, visit
www.MorganJamesBuilds.com.

Habitat
for Humanity®
Peninsula and
Greater Williamsburg
Building Partner

This is for the girls in the world who are afraid to let their true, awesome selves shine.

Have no fear, girls. We have your back.

All our best,
The Severson Sisters Team

Table of Contents

Foreword

Dear Super Girl,

The Severson Sisters Super Girl Guide To: Respect is a lighthearted and creative way to enhance self-respect while learning ways to develop stronger relationships among your peers. In the Severson Sisters Super Girl Guide To: Respect, you will also find a bullying-solution method that best fits what's going on in your life. We have a few different bullying-solution methods for you to choose from so that you can find the one that works best for you!

Self-esteem and creative arts are connected. Self-esteem and bullying are also connected. Severson Sisters is a nonprofit organization headquartered in Phoenix that created the connection between bullying solutions and creative arts.

This workbook is the first of six Severson Sisters will create. Each workbook will focus on a different theme. We'll eventually work on Acceptance, Relationships, Healthy Body Image, Peer Pressure, and Competition.

This first workbook is all about self-respect. The more self-respect you have, the less you'll be affected by bullying, and the less you'll want to bully someone. Most importantly, the more self-respect you have, the more confident you'll feel to help someone else out when you see bullying happening.

Self-respect is all about caring about yourself. In order to be nice and friendly to someone else, you have to treat yourself kindly first.

When Severson Sisters launched in January 2011 and started working with girls in Phoenix, we received requests from parents and teachers around the country asking for help.

This is our response. We hope you like it!

All our best Super Girl energy!

—The Severson Sisters

Acknowledgments

We have teachers, social workers, psychology experts, sisters, moms, dads, girls, business leaders, photographers, and editors invested in Severson Sisters. And this is my time to say THANK YOU!

First of all, to the real Severson Sisters, Holly: I'm grateful for every single thing you do to better my life and the lives of girls. To our Super Family: Thank you for giving so much to Severson Sisters. I'm so blessed you believed we could do this.

For months on end, the Severson Sisters Advisory Board wrote, brainstormed, laughed, and put so much energy into this project. Thank you to Holly, Shirley, Molly, Larissa, and Laura for bringing this workbook to life!

Thank you to Cansu Bulgu for our pretty pictures!

Thank you to Courtney Littler for your brilliant editing skills.

Thank you to Natalie Ehmka with Pretty Feisty Press and the entire Morgan James family for taking on Severson Sisters and this awesome project.

Thank you to the Board of Directors—Ed, Nicole, Suzanne, Laura, Amy, and Kristina—who embrace me and this awesome organization on a daily basis.

Thank you to Cristin Graham for believing in all things Super!

The most heartfelt thank you goes to you reading this. You're invested now, too, and we thank you very much for giving us the gift of your time and energy.

All my best Super Girl energy!

—Carrie Severson
Founder and CEO of Severson Sisters
Also…Totally a Super Girl

Introduction

The Severson Sisters Super Girl Guide To: RESPECT offers fun, creative activities that teach girls to give respect to themselves and to others.

Severson Sisters is a bullying solutions and self-compassion outreach program for girls based in Phoenix, Arizona. Severson Sisters works with girls to help them discover their super, awesome selves.

The Severson Sisters approach to bullying was developed specifically to meet the unique needs and interests of girls. Girls use very different tactics then boys do when they bully one another.

This creative curriculum focuses on infusing a positive energy into creative-arts lessons that demonstrate the fulfillment of positive behaviors.

Creative arts is a powerful tool for helping girls build self-respect, develop social skills to support healthy relationships, and see the power behind words and actions.

The Severson Sisters Super Girl Guide To: Respect utilizes best practices from social workers, educators, and psychology experts. Based on each girl's personality and experiences after completing this workbook, every Super Girl will have her very own action plan to help her the next time she is bullied, feels like bullying, or sees it happening to someone she cares about.

We think you should do this workbook with a Super Girl Supporter. Got that person ready? Good!

Get your Severson Sisters Super Girl going and have the best time!

CHAPTER

1

Ground Rules

We're so excited for you to begin! Follow this curriculum step-by-step to get the most out of the Severson Sisters program.

We have a few ground rules that we set with our girls before each program begins. We encourage you to do the same.

The ground rules are:

1. It's best to be open and honest. There is no judgment at any point in this workbook.
2. This program is lighthearted. Remember to turn on some fun music, and keep the positive energy going strong.
3. Enjoy every single second!
4. Get creative whenever you can.
5. Everyone MUST say her Super Girl Promise out loud and promise to follow through with it.

CHAPTER 2

The Timing of Super Girls

This workbook was written with the best of intentions. It should be a fun and positive learning experience for YOU about YOU.

We recommend that you do Super Girl Workbook chapters at different times. You'll see our break suggestions along the way. Take a 30-minute break, or take a few days. It's up to you. Just be sure to come back and continue working on your Super Girl!

If you feel like stopping before the next break, let your Super Girl Supporter know. Feel free to come back to that question or chapter at another time.

Severson Sisters!

CHAPTER 3

Meet Joy, Hope, and Grace

Dear Severson Sisters Super Girl,

My name is Joy, and I'm 12 years old. I'm in the middle of sixth grade, and so far I have all A's except for one B. My favorite subject in school is language arts. I like to write and read. My favorite kind of book is sci-fi and fantasy. I'm involved in student government and peer tutoring, and I've started a school-supplies drive for homeless kids.

My parents got divorced two years ago, and it was really tough. I live mostly with my mom, and I see my dad on the weekends. I have three younger brothers, and after my parents got divorced, I felt like I had to help my mom more around the house.

I had so much fun when I did this workbook with my mom. We haven't really had a lot of time to hang out by ourselves since the divorce. We spent an entire Saturday doing this workbook. It made it easier to talk to my mom about the stuff going on at school. I learned that my mom had some of the same problems when she was my age.

Girls make fun of me at school because I like to get good grades and I like to be the first to answer questions. I don't understand why that's a bad thing, but I'm called names sometimes and people steal my books at the lunch table. They gossip about me, too.

My favorite part about the Severson Sisters Super Girl Guide To: Respect was talking to my mom about what makes me special. It was not easy at first to open up to my mom, but after the first couple of questions, it got much better. I learned what I can do when I'm bullied at school. My bullying-solution method is Say It, Believe It, Repeat It.

I am a Super Girl because I'm smart, helpful and caring. And that's awesome.

Have fun!

Joy

Dear Severson Sisters Super Girl,

My name is Hope, and I'm in eighth grade. I just turned 14. I had a bunch of girls over for a sleepover, and there was a bunch of drama. I'm on a gymnastics team and in the drama club at school, so I have two different groups of friends. Well, I invited both of them to my birthday party. I didn't know that would be such a problem.

Halfway through the night, my gymnastics friends started being really mean to my drama club friends. Two of the gymnastic girls gossiped all night about one of my favorite drama club friends. I felt pressured into picking sides. Because my drama club is at school, I had to choose that side. So I didn't talk to my gymnastics friends the rest of the night or say good-bye to them the next morning. I made fun of the two girls who were being the meanest, and they overheard me.

When I go to gymnastics now, I feel left out. Nobody talks to me. My dad came to pick me up one night from gymnastics, and I was crying. I told him everything that happened at my party and what it's been like since then.

My dad bought me the Severson Sisters Super Girl Guide To: Respect as a way to help me figure out what I should do the next time I go to gymnastics.

The activities in the workbook made me see what I did wrong the night of my birthday party. I want to be a nice person to everyone. Now I know what I can do differently. Things have gotten better with my friends since I did the Severson Sisters Super Girl Guide To: Respect.

My favorite part was reading through all the different bullying-solution methods and learning how to be friends with everyone. I didn't know how to deal with the drama at my birthday party, but I will know next time.

I have two bullying-solution methods. One is Find Your Inner Peace and the other is Friends Unite. I'm a Super Girl because I'm playful, fun, and friendly.

Why are you a Super Girl?

Hope

Dear Severson Sisters Super Girl,

I'm Grace. I'm in fifth grade. I'm 10 years old, and I live with my grandma and grandpa. I moved in with them when I was in kindergarten. My mom got sick and I didn't know my dad. My grandma and grandpa take good care of me.

My grandma thought the Severson Sisters Super Girl Guide To: Respect would be good for me to do with her. I'm made fun of sometimes because of how I dress. We don't have a lot of money, so I wear used clothes. Some kids who don't know me ask a lot of questions about why I don't have a mom and dad.

I help my grandma and grandpa at home by drying the dishes. I help my grandpa around the house because he uses a cane.

I'm in the art club, and I love to draw butterflies. My best grade is in art. I always get an A. My favorite thing to do at home is baking cookies with my grandma. I like to give my cookies to my friends because it makes them smile. I also like to make my friends homemade birthday cards and write them notes when they're having bad days.

My grandma and I did this workbook on Sunday. We had a lot of fun. I really liked the art activities. There's a butterfly, a heart, a shield, and a star you get to decorate any way you want to. We even took a break and made our cookies.

Even though I'm nice to everyone and give out cookies and notes, my feelings still get hurt when I'm made fun of. I learned how to feel better when some kids are really mean after I finished the Severson Sisters Super Girl Guide To: Respect.

My bullying-solution method is Speak Up Super Girl! I am a Super Girl because I'm giving, caring, and creative.

I know you're going to have so much doing this.

Have fun making your artwork.

Grace

What You Can Expect During the Severson Sisters Super Girl Guide To:

CHAPTER 4

Respect

What did Joy, Hope, and Grace experience when they went through the Severson Sisters Super Girl Guide To: RESPECT?

Joy:

1. My mom and I did this workbook over a few weekends. I have a lot of homework, so I did this workbook when I needed a homework break. I liked the creating parts.
2. I learned how to journal, and now I journal every day after school.

Hope:

1. After the workbook, I told my friends about all the cool activities in the workbook. They came over to my house to see what I wrote down about why I think I'm a Super Girl.
2. I learned that I act as a bystander too much. I learned what to do next time I see a friend bullying another friend.

Grace:

1. My grandma and I did this workbook in one Saturday, and it was a lot of fun.
2. Some questions in this workbook were hard for me to answer. I took my time and took more breaks than the workbook had.

CHAPTER
5

Confidence Star Policy

We ask you to remember our five key points as you enjoy this workbook: Safety, Honesty, Creativity, Openness, and Fun.

Please sign your name in the middle of your Confidence Star and keep it near you as you complete this workbook.

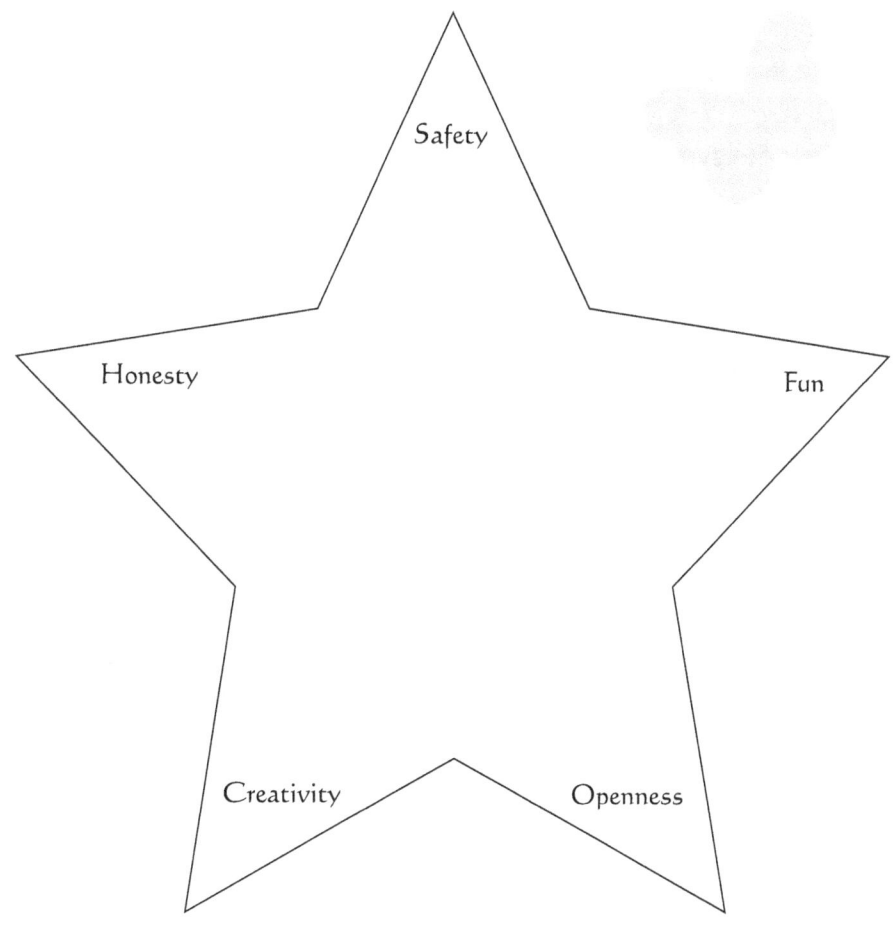

CHAPTER

6

Ways to Be Creative throughout the Workbook

You'll need to grab a few things before you start.

Check off these items:

___ Scissors

___ Construction paper

___ Markers, crayons, or colored pencils

___ Glitter

___ Favorite symbols

___ Favorite photos or paintings

___ Take a trip to a local craft store and focus on colors that make you smile.

___ Grab a special journal

___ Get a pen!

Get ready to have a lot of fun!

CHAPTER 7

What Does Your Severson Sisters Super Girl Look Like?

Get ready to discover the Super Girl within YOU. Part of this is defining what a Super Girl looks like.

Here are the Super Girl definitions of Joy, Grace, and Hope.
Joy: I can handle a lot of things and keep my cool.
Grace: I am accepting of others and I appreciate what I have in life.
Hope: A Super Girl is always finding the fun in every situation.

Why are you a Super Girl?

Here are ways Joy, Grace, and Hope respect themselves.
Joy: I'm an awesome reader. I read a book a month just for fun.
Grace: I love to bake. I'm a big helper around the kitchen.
Hope: I smile at people in the hallway even if they don't smile back.

Write down three reasons you respect yourself.

CHAPTER 8

Goals

To start the Severson Sisters Super Girl Guide To: RESPECT, we ask that you set your goals for your workbook.

This can be anything you want. Here are Joy's, Grace's, and Hope's goals for themselves as they went through the workbook.

Joy: My goal is to be open and honest with myself.

Hope: My goal is to have fun and learn how to make more friends.

Grace: My goal is to be kind and patient with myself.

We want you to write down three goals and say them out loud.

1.

2.

3.

Once you've set your goals for the workbook, cut out the Severson Sisters Super Girl Promises on the next three pages and read one out loud.

SUPER GIRL
Promise

I promise to say "I am unique and there is only one me. I'm the best at being me"

SUPER GIRL
Promise

I promise to close my eyes and think about something that made me proud today

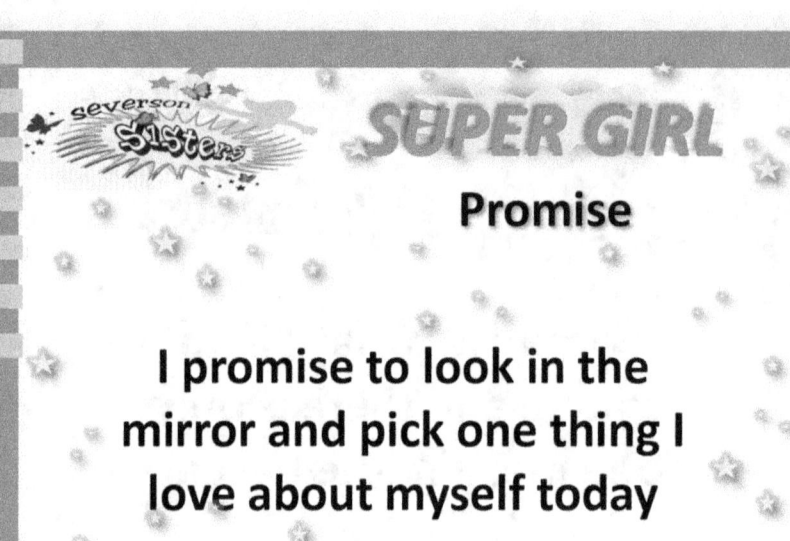

SUPER GIRL

Promise

I promise to look in the mirror and tell myself I'm pretty today

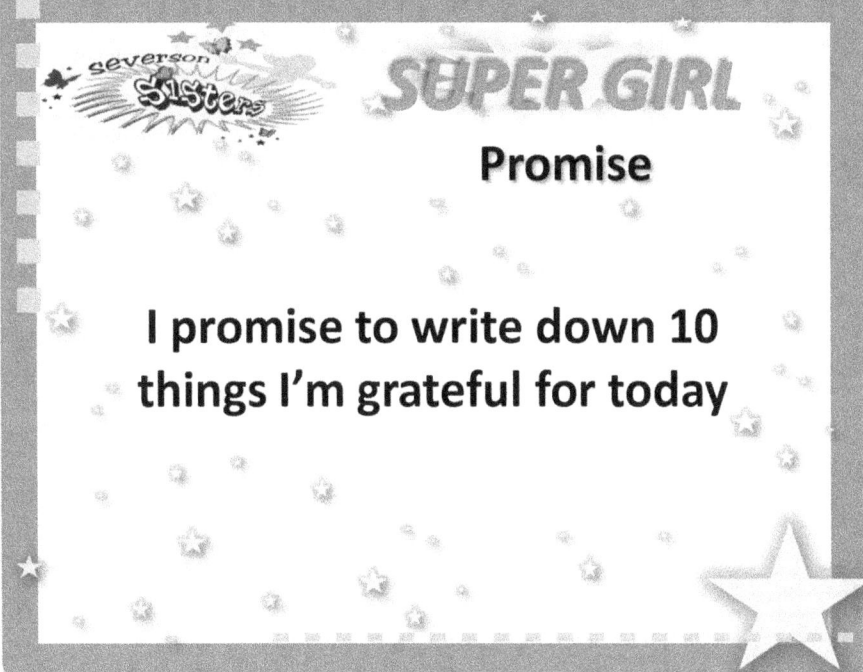

SUPER GIRL

Promise

I promise to write down 10 things I'm grateful for today

SUPER GIRL

Promise

I promise to do something super-duper fun just for me today

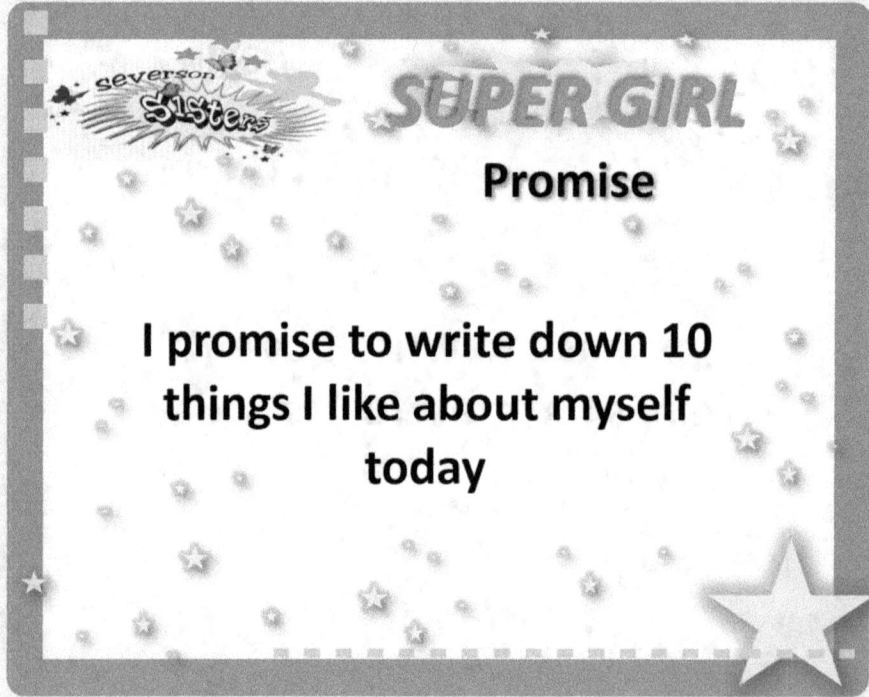

SUPER GIRL

Promise

I promise to write down 10 things I like about myself today

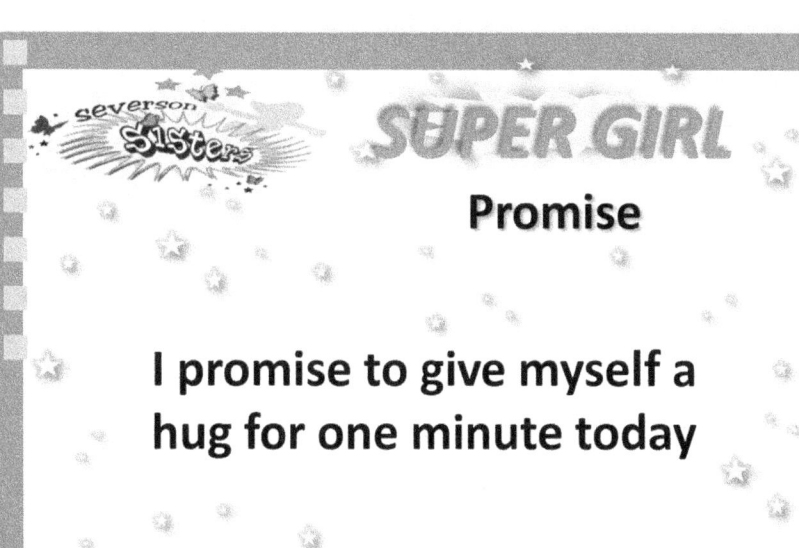

SUPER GIRL

Promise

I promise to give myself a hug for one minute today

SUPER GIRL

Promise

I promise use only positive and kind words when talking about myself today

Take a break, Super Girl!

Come back and pick this
up when you're able to.

You're doing GREAT!

CHAPTER

9

Gems and Shapes

On the next few pages, you'll find some fun gem shapes for you to color and cut out. Once you're done, use the gems to decorate the front page of this workbook. Be sure to take a picture of your work!

As you decorate, your Super Girl Supporter is going to ask you the questions below. Have your Super Girl Supporter write down your answers here as you decorate.

A. What's your theme song?

B. What do those words mean to you?

C. What is the coolest part of your year so far?

D. What's your least favorite part of your year?

E. What are you excited about or looking forward to next school year?

F.   What things (if any) worry you about next school year?

G.   What are some things that you are grateful for in your life?

H.   What's your favorite TV show?

I.   What does that TV show mean to you?

J.   If you could invite one person to dinner, who would it be and why?

K.   If you could invent one thing, what would it be?

L.   If you could have one Super Girl Power, what would it be and why?

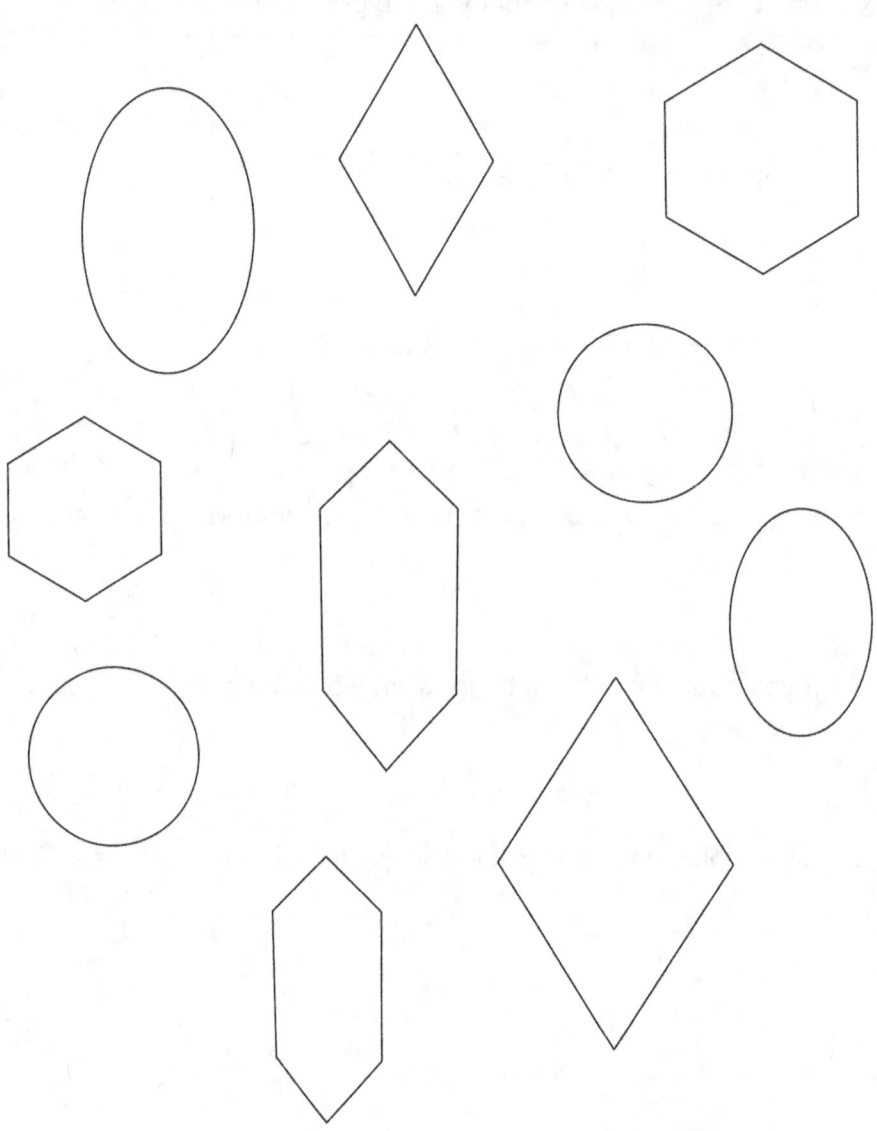

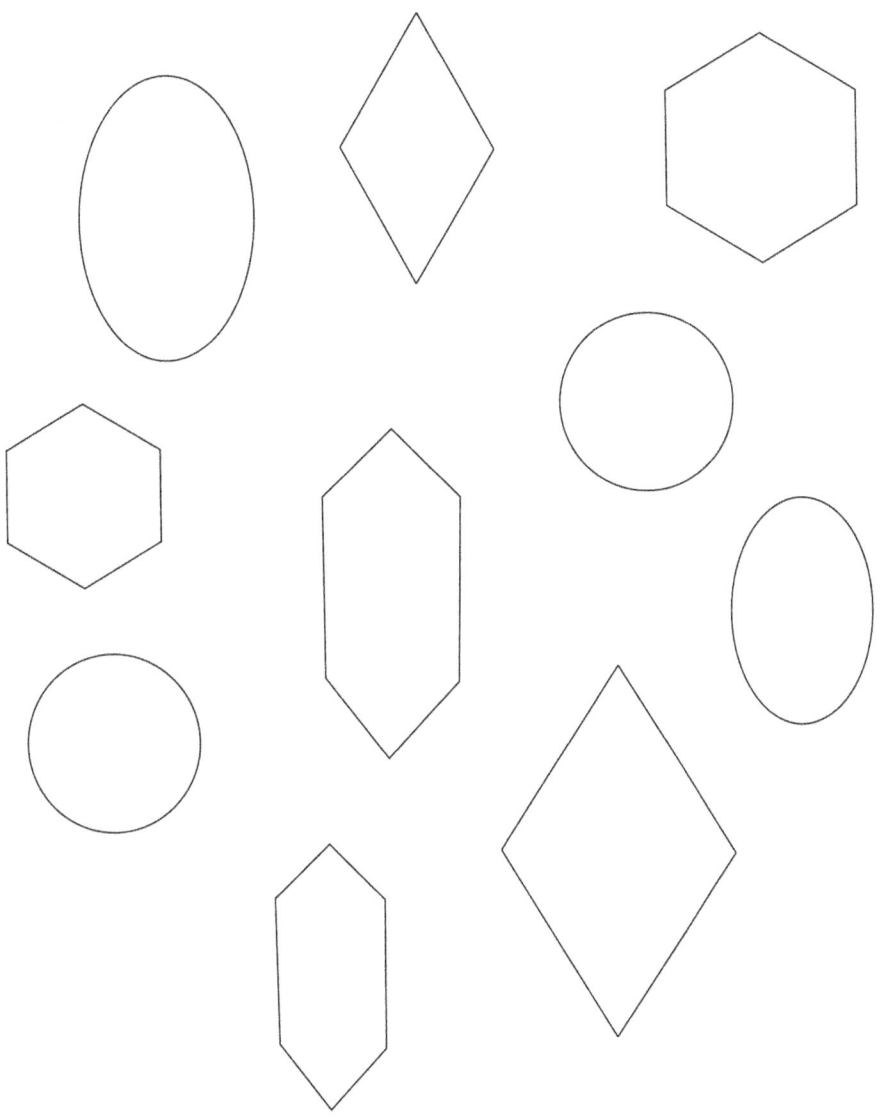

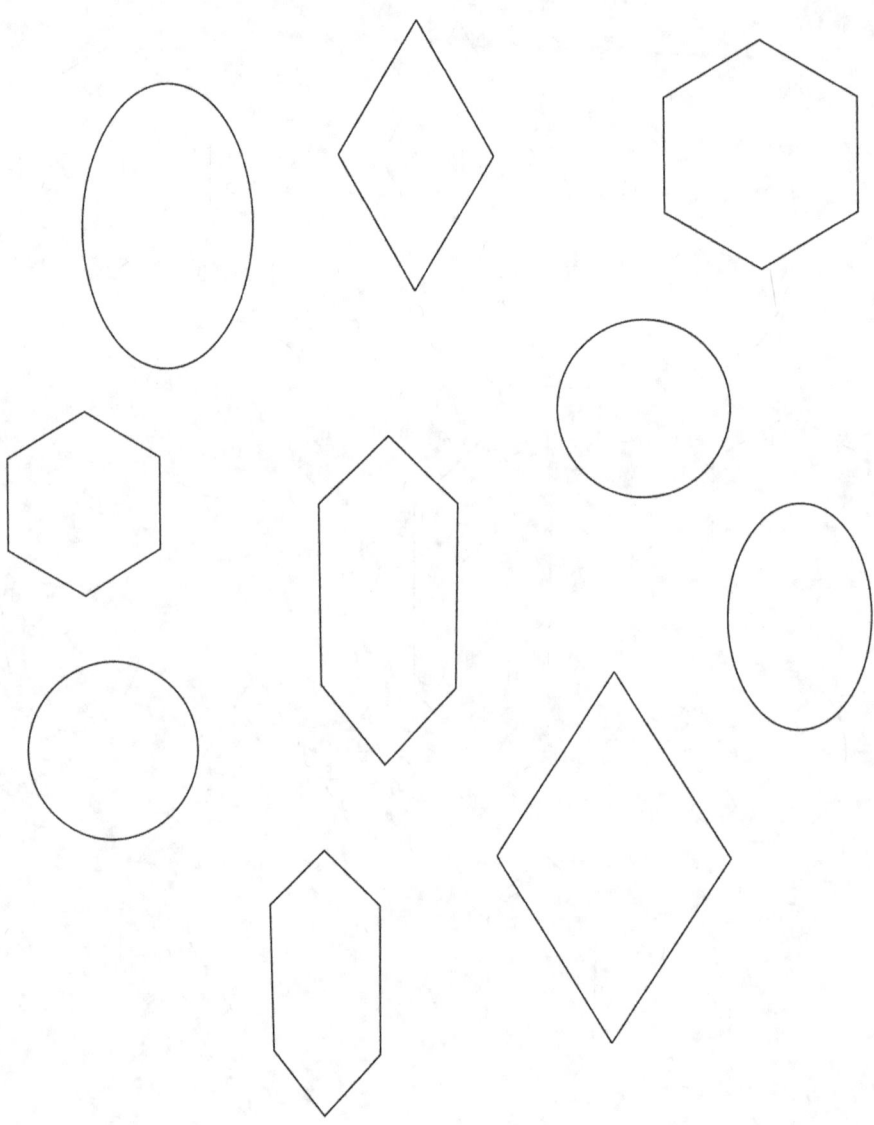

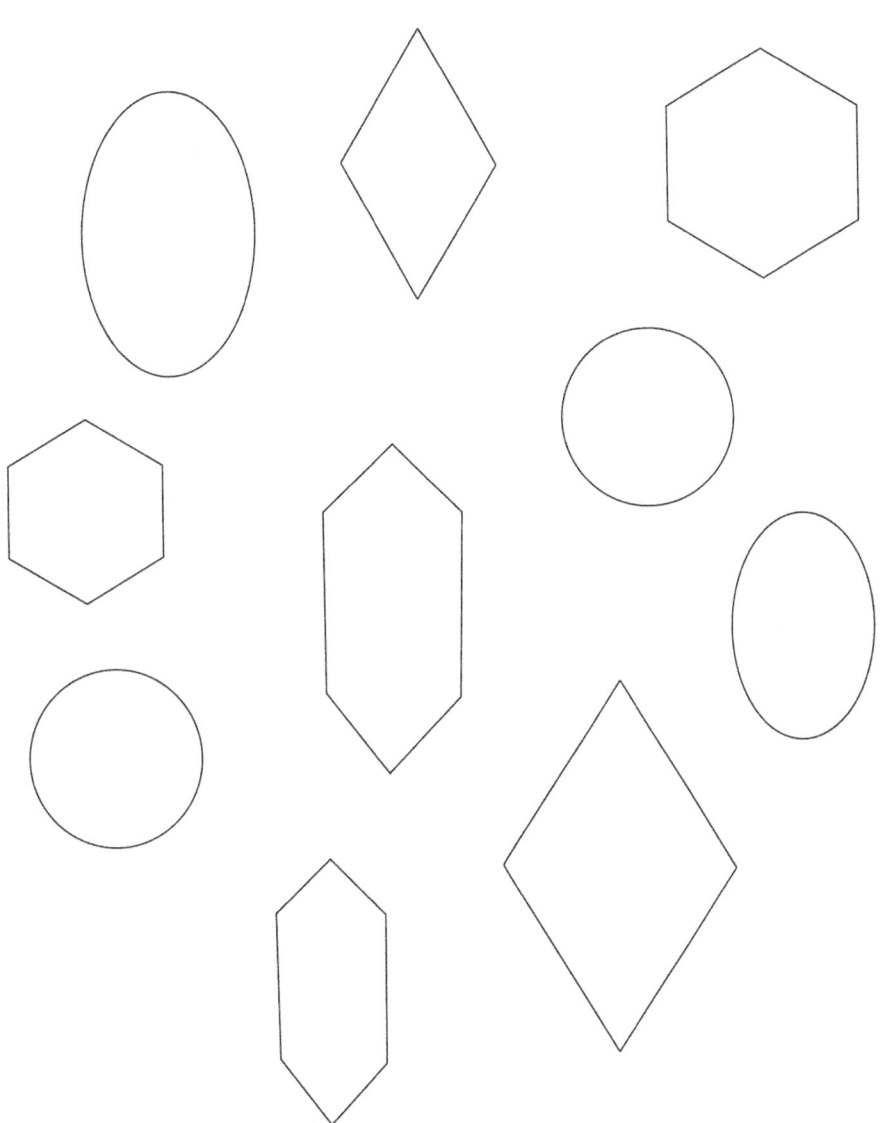

CHAPTER
10

All About YOU!

This chapter is all about you! Answer these questions as honestly as you can.

1. Name three things kids in your grade could do that show they respect themselves.

2. Write down three ways you are special.

3. What do you do to feel special or fit in at school?
   Joy says: I am always the first one to answer questions and I do all the extra credit.
   Hope says: I like to try out for the lead in the school play.
   Grace says: I bring my grandma's chocolate chip cookies to my friends for their birthday.

4. List names kids at school call you. Describe how those names make you feel.

    Names that give me good feelings:

    Names that give me bad feelings:

5. Name five people you see in magazines, movies, or on TV you want to be like. Why do you want to be like them?

6. Have there ever been times when you put yourself down?

   Joy says: I feel bad about myself when I get a bad grade.
   Hope says: I feel bad when I don't get a medal in a gymnastics
   meet.
   Grace says: I feel bad when I'm asked to bring my mom or dad
   to school events.

7. List three positive qualities that people have.

8. List three negatives qualities that people have.

9. What do you most like about yourself? List five things here.

Take a break, Super Girl!

Come back and pick this
up when you're able to.

You're doing GREAT!

CHAPTER

11

Power Words

Now it's time to find your POWER Words. Circle 10 words that best describe you. These words are now known as your Power Words!

Courageous	Positive	Understanding
Strong	Intelligent	Motivated
Loving	Enthusiastic	Genuine
Powerful	Creative	Graceful
Respectful	Grateful	Faithful
Sophisticated	Successful	Leader
Calm	Determined	Trusting
Loyal	Friendly	Patient
Fun	Feminine	Supportive
Confident	Trustworthy	Independent
Steady	Mature	Energetic
Healthy	Beautiful	Playful
Peaceful	Funny	Empowered
Optimistic	Athletic	Forgiving
Joyful	Witty	Honorable
Talented	Wonderful	Unique

CHAPTER 12

Butterfly, Star, Heart, Shield Words

Cut out **ONE OF EACH** Butterfly, Heart, Shield, and Star from the next pages. Write your 10 Power Words on each image, and decorate the images. Get creative! There are no rules. Be sure to take pictures of your work!

Check out Hope's, Joy's, and Grace's work on the next pages, too!

As you decorate your Butterfly, Star, Heart, and Shield, your Super Girl Supporter is going to ask you questions at the end of this chapter, so it may be helpful for you to hand over the workbook to your Super Girl Supporter after you cut out your shapes.

HOPE STAR

JOY STAR

GRACE STAR

HOPE HEART

JOY HEART

GRACE HEART

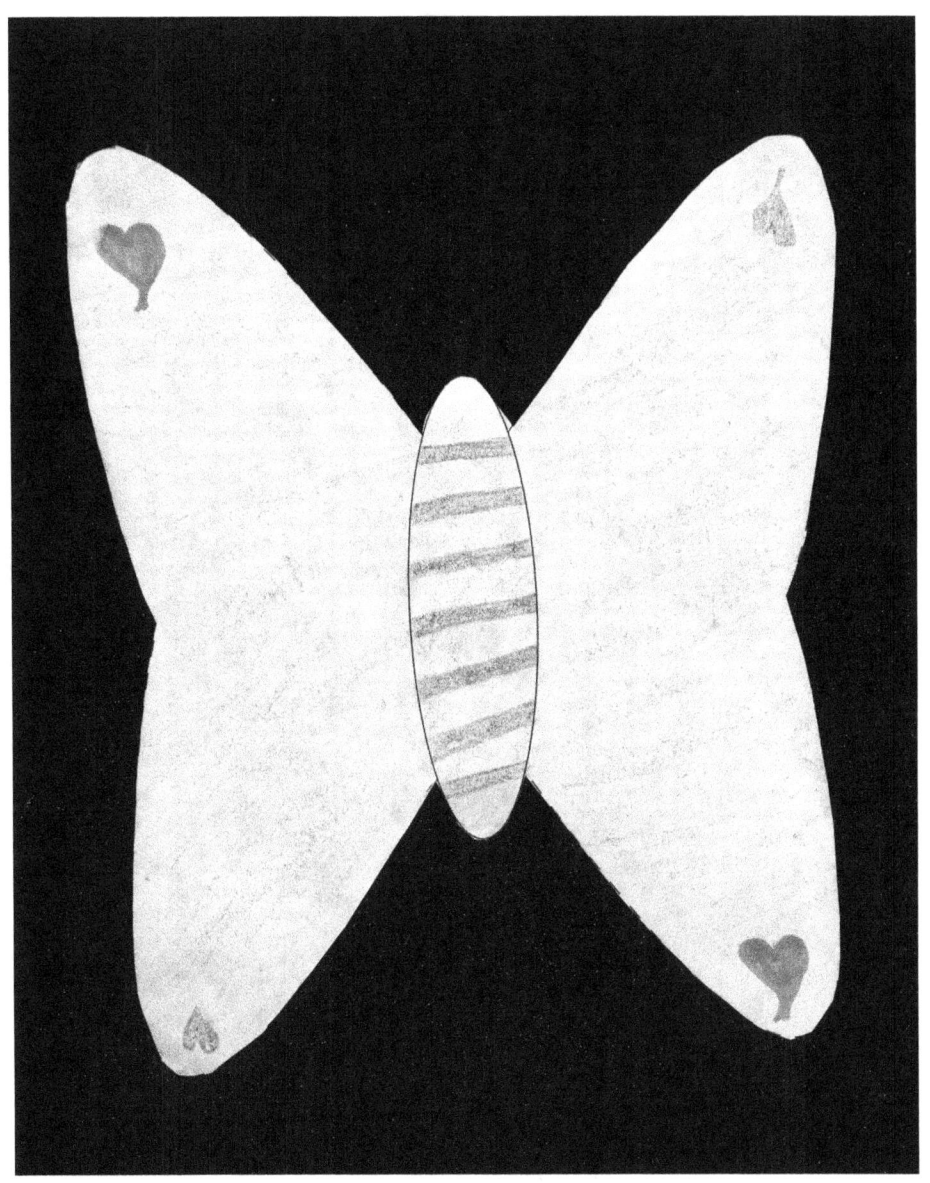

HOPE BUTTERFLY

JOY BUTTERFLY

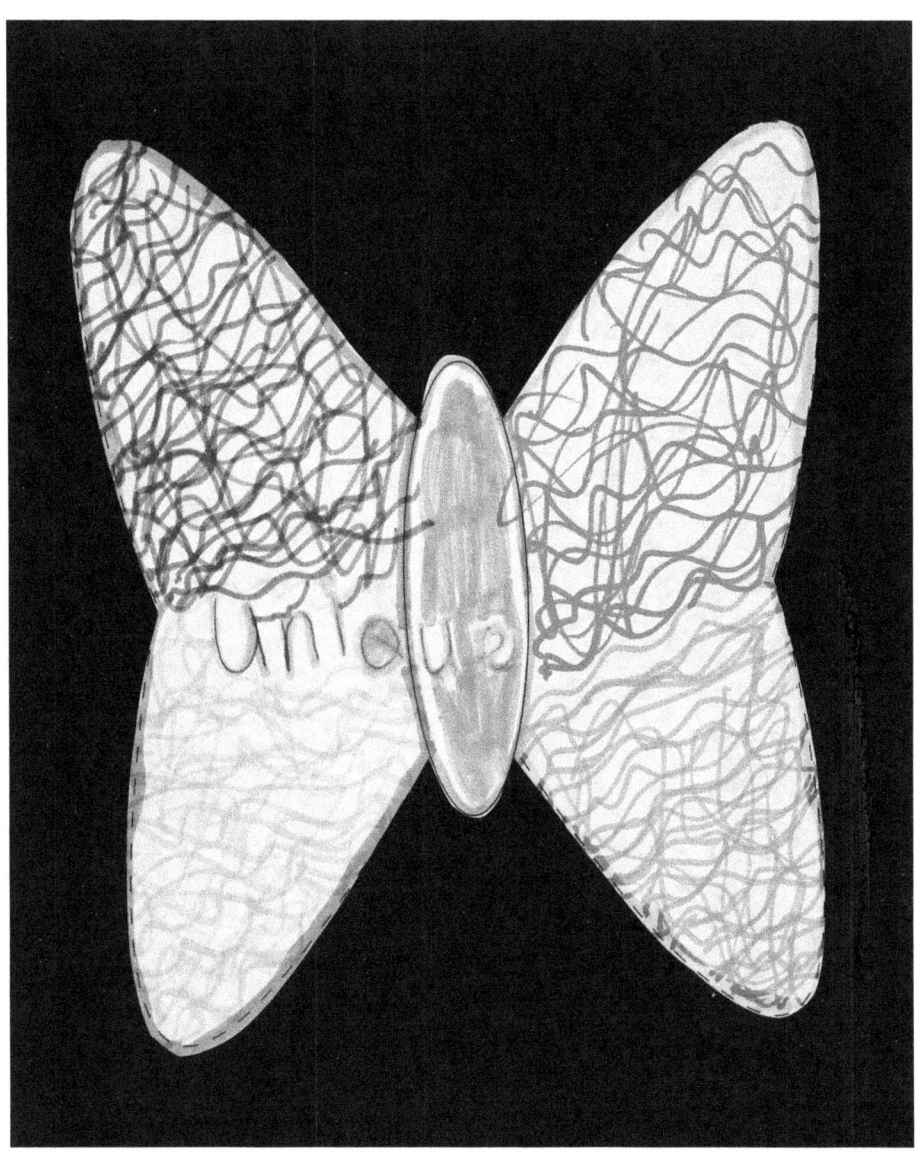

GRACE BUTTERFLY

HOPE SHIELD

JOY SHIELD

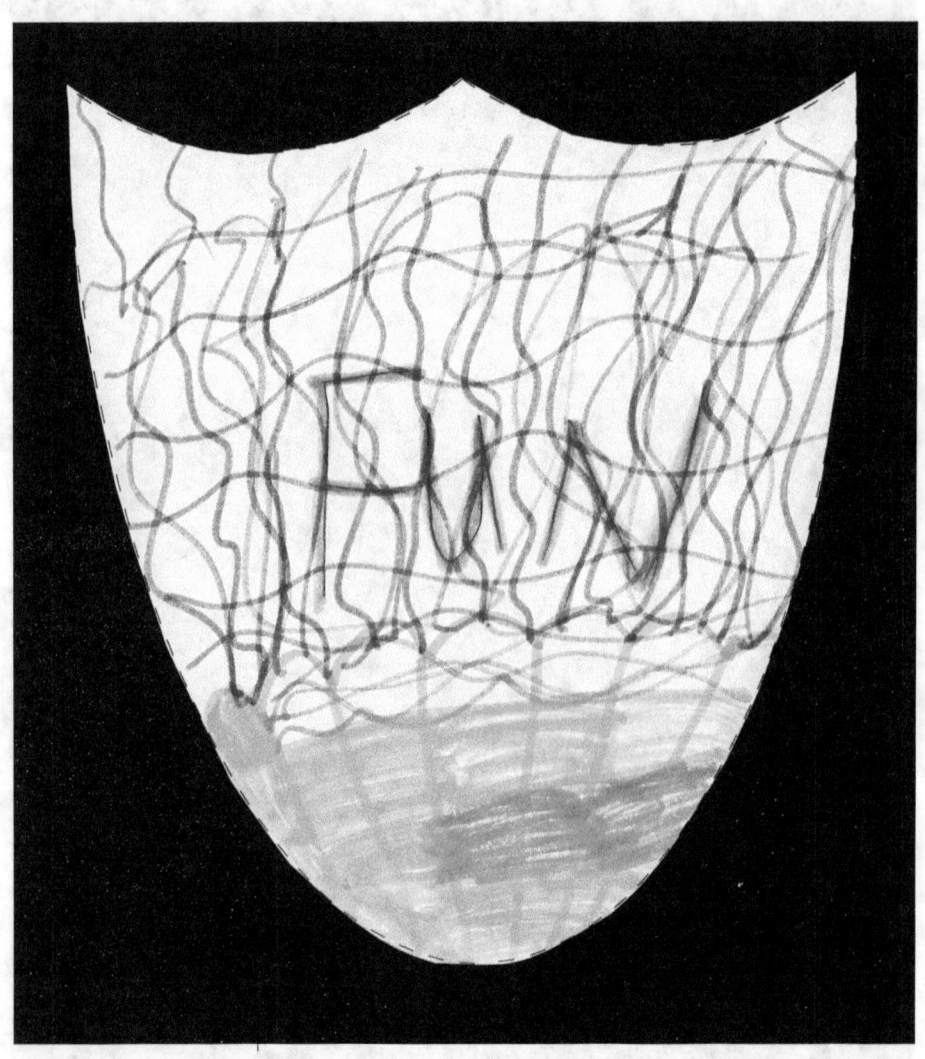

GRACE SHIELD

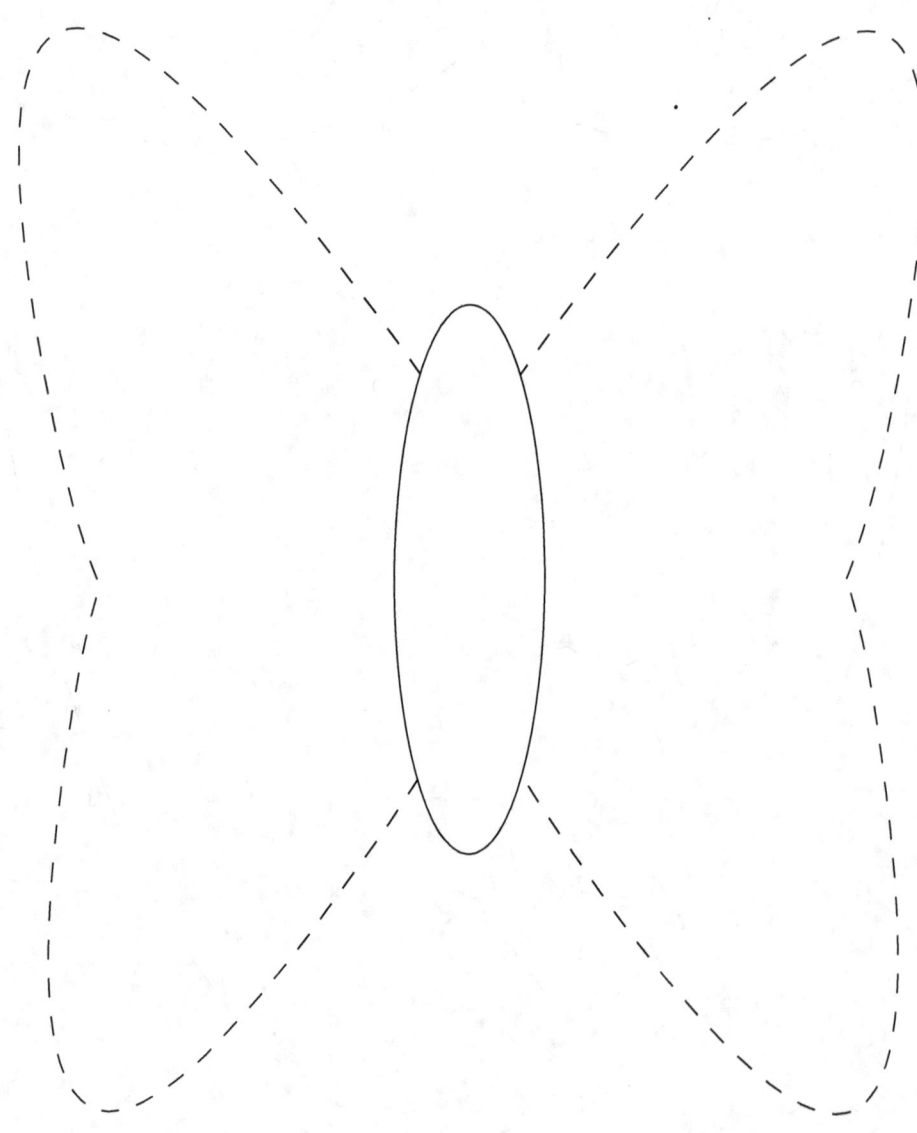

Dear Super Girl Supporter,

You're up!

While your Super Girl is creating fun, loving shapes filled with Power Words, use this time to discuss situations about self-respect and bullying.

It's important for the Super Girls to communicate while they are creating. On the next four pages, we provide questions you can ask your Super Girl while she's creating.

Let her talk. When you hear an opening to lead a conversation about popularity, arguments, or bullying, do so.

In our program, it's been our experience that the girls will find answers to their own questions. They sometimes welcome a light on the path, and that's where you come in.

We've heard amazing results from this portion of our program. Girls have learned what true friendship is all about. We've heard some girls come up with positive messages they repeat to themselves when they encounter a bully.

When you do encounter some touchy topics, we're happy to help you navigate your way through.

Here are some messages from our Advisory Board members to help you.

1. When talking about bullying, peer pressure, or popularity, ask your Super Girl to think about the situation from someone else's viewpoint.
2. How does your Super Girl think her other friends might be feeling about the situations she's bringing up during creative time?
3. Ask your Super Girl, "What advice would you give to a friend in this situation?"

Write down notes to these answers as your Super Girl is busy creating. Ready? Go!

    a. What are some of the most important traits that your friends would say you have? Are you proud of those traits? Why?

    b. What friends do you associate with your Power Words?

    c. What do you value about your friendships?

d. Where's your happy place?

e. What activities are you interested in trying that could show your creativity?

f. What would the cover of your autobiography look like if it could not be a picture of you or your family?

g. If you could change any one thing about yourself, what would it be? Why would you change it?

h. Who do you sit with at lunch? Is that person or are those people kind to you? Are you kind to them?

i. Describe the most beautiful thing you have ever seen.

j. If you could be a famous athlete, actor, writer, or musician, who would you be and why?

k. If you had to give every human being one quality, what would it be and why?

l. What are some qualities that you think are most important in being a friend? How would you rank these qualities (1st, 2nd, 3rd)?

m. What makes people be mean to others?

n. What can you do if somebody is being mean to someone else?

Take a break, Super Girl!

Come back and pick this
up when you're able to.

You're doing GREAT!

 **CHAPTER 13**

Butterfly, Star, Heart, Shield Pictures

Now cut out the other Butterfly, Star, Heart, and Shield on the next few pages. On these shapes, draw images that relate to your Power Words. For example: If your word is Loving, do you think of a heart? Draw a heart! Do you think of a flower? Draw a flower! Get creative and take pictures of your work.

As you decorate your next Butterfly, Star, Heart, and Shield, your Super Girl Supporter is going to ask you questions at the end of this chapter. Go ahead and hand over the workbook to your Super Girl Supporter after you cut out your shapes.

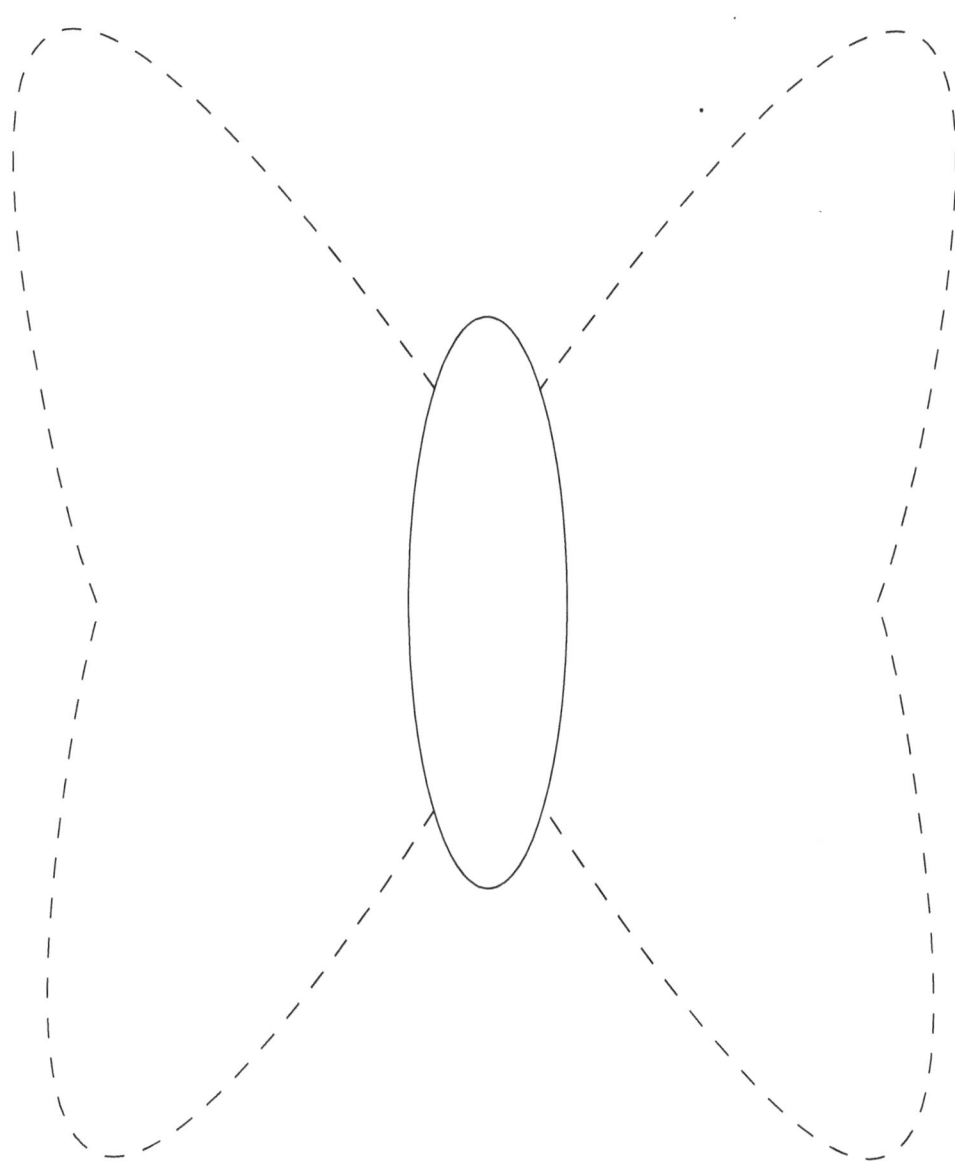

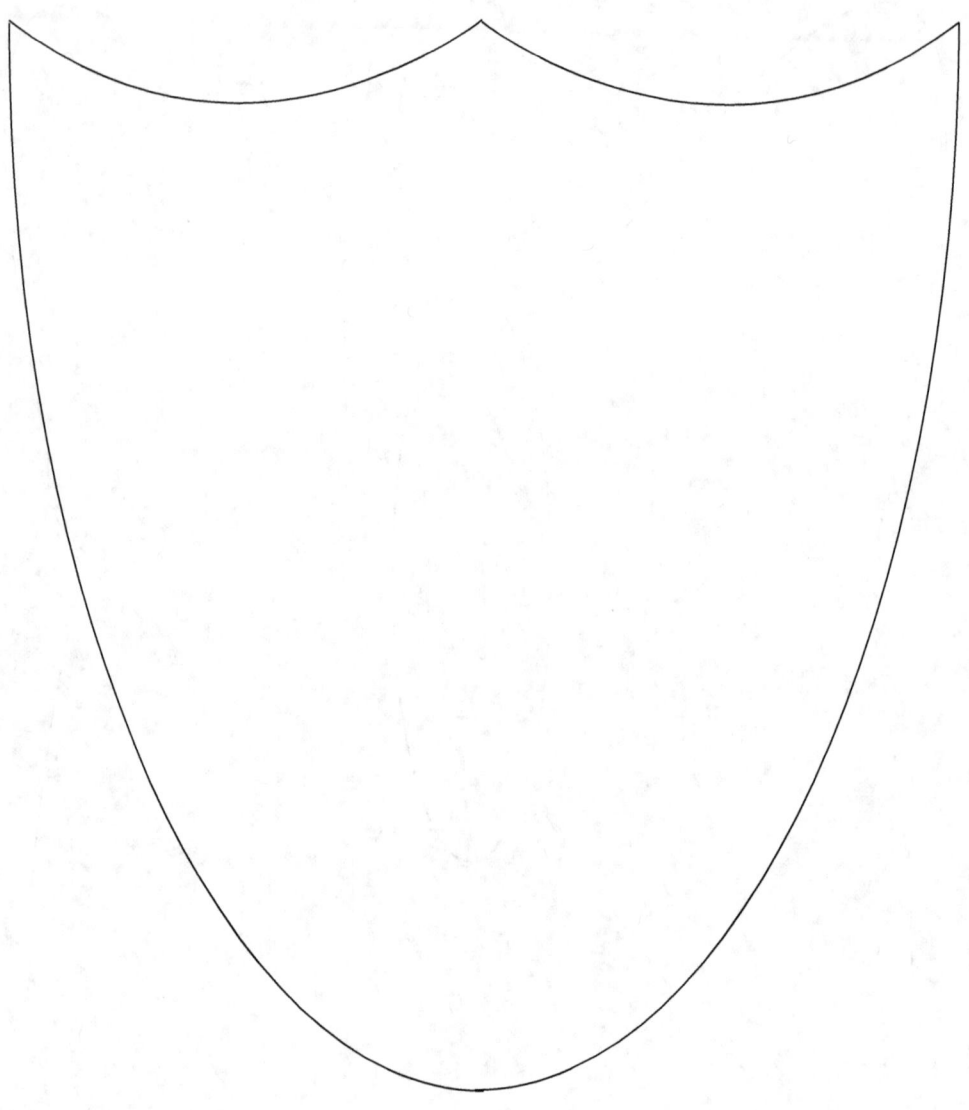

Dear Super Girl Supporter,

You're doing an awesome job! We hope you're enjoying this experience. You're going to continue the conversation about self-respect and bullying.

It's important for Super Girls to communicate while they are creating. On the next four pages, we provide questions you can ask your Super Girl while she's creating.

Let her talk. When you hear an opening to lead a conversation about popularity, arguments, or bullying, do so.

We're providing these questions to create an open dialogue with your Super Girl about her self-esteem. It's up to you to decide what to do with this information based on what works for your family.

These questions are the ones we ask when we are personally working with girls.

Write down notes to these answers as your Super Girl is busy creating. Ready? Go!

a. What things would you change at school if you could?

b. If you were running for president of your school, what rules would you make or change? As school president, how could you help others get along better and have less bullying?

c. Do you see bullying as a problem at your school?

d. Who are the top three most important people in your life?

e. If you could know one thing about the future, what would it be? Why is it important that you know it?

f. What is the meanest thing someone could say to you? What is the best thing someone could say to you?

g. How was the last argument you had resolved?

h. Has anyone ever said anything mean to you at school or on the bus? If so, what was it? Did you say anything back? If so, what did you say? Did you stand up for yourself? If so, how?

i. Did you tell a teacher? If so, what did you tell that teacher? What did the teacher do? Did you walk away? Did you find your friends?

j. Have you ever said anything mean to someone at school or on the bus? If so, what did you say and why did you say it?

k. What made you say it? Did your friends encourage you? If so, what reaction did you get from your friends?

l. Would you rather be the girl being bullied or the girl doing the bullying? Why?

Take a break, Super Girl!

Come back and pick this
up when you're able to.

You're doing GREAT!

CHAPTER
14

True or False?

Answer these questions. Your Super Girl Supporter can find the answers to the first three questions on the Severson Sisters website.

1. One out of three children are bullied regularly nationwide. True or False?

2. Girls spread rumors more than boys. True or False?

3. Bullying happens most often in middle school. True or False?

4. I stepped in for a friend when he/she was being bullied. True or False?

5. I've said something that has hurt someone's feelings before. True or False?

6. I've watched and not done anything when a friend was being bullied. True or False?

7. I trust my teacher to do something when bullying happens. True or False?

8. I felt bad about myself because of something a close friend said about me. True or False?

9. I spread rumors. True or False?

10. I've stopped being friends with someone because it was the cool thing to do. True or False?

Take a break, Super Girl!

Come back and pick this
up when you're able to.

You're doing GREAT!

Dear Severson Sisters
Super Girl

Here are a few situations that we heard about. Read through these. Do you agree with the answer? We have a few questions for you to answer yourself, too.

Dear Severson Sisters Super Girl,

My friend is nice to me one day and mean to me the next. Is this a true friend? What should I do?

Signed,
Confused

Dear Confused,

Well, it is definitely not fair that your friend treats you well on some days and treats you poorly on other days. It's possible that your friend does not know exactly what she is doing and how it's making you feel. Sometimes she may just be having a bad day, and taking it out on you. You may want to brainstorm ways to let her know how she is making you feel. Perhaps you could just sit down with her one day and let her know how it makes you feel when she treats you badly. It is always good to use "I" statements so she doesn't feel like you are criticizing her. Explain to your friend, "I feel hurt when you treat me badly on some days." When she is nice to you, tell her you are glad you're friends with her. If she is a true friend, she will see how poorly she's treating you on some days and change her behavior. It's up to you to speak your mind, though. Let her know how you feel.

Hope that helps!
Severson Sisters Super Girl

Dear Severson Sisters Super Girl,

I want to make new friends, but I don't know how to. What do you think I should do?

Signed,
Looking for new friends

Dear Looking for new friends,

For starters, a smile and a "hello" can go a really long way. It's also good to get involved with activities at your school, like a sports team, art club, or the student council. Think about some ideas for striking up a good conversation. Ask the other person what things they like to do, or what TV shows or movies they watch. Also, think about the things you have in common with the other person. For example, if you have the same math teacher, you might say, "Wow, was it just me, or did you think that math homework was hard last night?" Are you waiting for people to come up to start the conversation? Don't be shy! Put a smile on and let people know you're a super cool girl! Be nice, get involved with a club or activity you like, and you'll make friends super quick!

Hope that helps!
Severson Sisters Super Girl

Here are some questions for you to answer on your own!

Dear Severson Sisters Super Girl,

I saw two girls gossiping about me. What do I do about it?

Signed,
Hurt

Dear Hurt,

Dear Severson Sisters Super Girl,

Is it important to be in one group of friends or is it okay to be in few different groups?

Signed,
Don't want to choose

Dear Don't want to choose,

CHAPTER 16

Bullying Situations

Severson Sisters helps girls find the right approach to handle bullying situations. Answer these questions honestly to best help find the right action plan for you.

1. Have you ever wanted to hurt someone when you've been angry or frustrated? Explain the situation.

2. Have you ever left someone out on purpose? Explain the situation.

3. Have you ever used your cell phone or computer to spread rumors or hurt someone's feelings on purpose?

4. Have you ever witnessed someone being bullied and not stepped in? Did you think someone else was going to step in?

5. Did you think you'd lose friends for stepping in when witnessing someone being bullied?

6. Did you think you'd be bullied yourself for stepping in when someone else was being bullied?

7. Do you feel the other kids at school mistreat you for reasons you don't understand? Why do you think you are mistreated?

8. Are you called names often? If so, what are you called?

9. Do you feel safe going to school or walking in the hallways at school?

The exercises you just went through will help you identify with one of three different roles. Circle the role you think you fit in.

a. The girl experiencing the bullying firsthand.
b. The girl doing the bullying.
c. The girl witnessing the bullying happening as a bystander.

It's possible that you could benefit from one, two, or even all three bullying-solution methods. In the next chapter, we'll show you nine different bullying-solution methods.

Take a break, Super Girl!

Come back and pick this
up when you're able to.

You're doing GREAT!

Bullying-Solution Method Action Plan for Option A

Next, let's map out your action plan to help you navigate your way when you're being bullied at school. Answer these three questions to determine which Bullying-Solution Method Action Plan best works for you. We suggest you review all three methods so you can practice them all.

1. Do you feel comfortable saying something to someone when he or she is bullying you? If so, what have you said to someone as you've been bullied?

2. Do you feel more comfortable walking away from someone when he or she is bullying you without saying anything at all? If so, what do you do after you walk away?

3. Do you feel better surrounded by a group of friends when someone or a group of people are bullying you? If so, who do you turn to for help?

If you said yes to question 1, your Bullying-Solution Method is Speak Up Super Girl.

If you said yes to question 2, your Bullying-Solution Method is Say It, Believe It, Repeat It.

If you said yes to question 3, your Bullying-Solution Method is Friends Unite.

Speak Up Super Girl!

★ Write down three short, confident statements below that you will say to a bully, such as "**That isn't funny**" or "**I don't appreciate what you are doing.**"

_____

_____

_____

★ If somebody bullies you, say the three sentences you wrote above. Look directly at the bully. Say the sentences clearly. Then confidently walk away.

★ Tell a teacher or another adult you trust about what happened. Let this person know who bullied you and what the bully said.

★ Next, be sure to tell your parent or guardian what happened. Tell them who was involved and what was said.

★ Take out your journal. Answer these questions:
   1. How did you feel when you were bullied?
   2. How did you feel when you responded to this person?
   3. How do you feel now?
   4. Do you need to talk more about what happened? If you do, tell your parent or guardian.

★ **FORGIVE YOUR BULLY!** Get creative here. Write a forgiveness letter or a card to the person who bullied you. You don't have to show your bully this letter or card. This is just for you. In the letter or card, **write down** and **say** the following lines **out loud:**
   1. I forgive you for what happened today.
   2. I understand what you're going through is hard for you.
   3. I know that what you did today had nothing to do with me.

Say It, Believe It, Repeat It

★ Write down three short "**I am**" statements below. What makes you a Super Girl? Examples: "**I am LOVING**" or "**I am PRETTY**" or "**I am CREATIVE.**"

_____

_____

_____

★ If somebody bullies you, calmly and confidently walk away. While walking away, repeat the "**I am**" statements you wrote above. Say each statement to yourself **THREE** times.

★ Tell a teacher or another adult you trust about what happened. Let this person know who bullied you and what the bully said.

★ Next, be sure to tell your parent or guardian what happened. Tell them who was involved and what was said.

★ Take out your journal. Answer these questions:
  1. How did you feel when you were bullied?
  2. How did you feel when you responded to this person?
  3. How do you feel now?
  4. Do you need to talk more about what happened? If you do, tell your parent or guardian.

★ **FORGIVE YOUR BULLY!** Get creative here. Write a forgiveness letter or a card to the person who bullied you. You don't have to show your bully this letter or card. This is just for you. In the letter or card, **write down** and **say** the following lines **out loud:**
  1. I forgive you for what happened today.
  2. I understand what you're going through is hard for you.
  3. I know that what you did today had nothing to do with me.

FRIENDS UNITE

★ When you see a bully, confidently and calmly walk to your friends. Let them know you need their support. Tell your friends to stay cool so that the situation does not escalate. Your friends can say things like, "**Please don't talk to my friend like that.**" Or, "**Leave us alone.**"

★ Tell a teacher or another adult you trust about what happened. Let this person know who bullied you and what the bully said.

★ Next, be sure to tell your parent or guardian what happened. Tell them who was involved and what was said.

★ Take out your journal. Answer these questions:
  1. How did you feel when you were bullied?
  2. How did you feel when you responded to this person?
  3. How do you feel now?
  4. Do you need to talk more about what happened? If you do, tell your parent or guardian.

★ **FORGIVE YOUR BULLY!** Get creative here. Write a forgiveness letter or card to the person who bullied you. You have to show your bully this letter or card. This is just for you. In the letter or card, **write down** and **say** the following lines **out loud:**
  1. I forgive you for what happened today.
  2. I understand what you're going through is hard for you.
  3. I know that what you did today had nothing to do with me.

CHAPTER
18

Bullying-Solution
Methods for Option B

This chapter will help you figure out your action plan when you feel like you have to bully someone to feel good about yourself. Answer these three questions to determine which Bullying-Solution Method Action Plan best works for you. We suggest you review all three methods so you can practice them all.

1. What happens when you pick on someone? How does this make you feel?

2. Do you get frustrated at school a lot? Do you ever feel like you are not able to meet expectations at school?

3. Do you feel as though you are treated poorly? In a perfect day, how would everyone in the world be treated every day?

If you have more to say to question 1, your Bullying-Solution Method is Find Your Inner Peace.

If you have more to say to question 2, your Bullying-Solution Method is Break the Cycle.

If you have more to say to question 3, your Bullying-Solution Method is Treat Others the Way You Want to Be Treated.

Find Your Inner Peace

★ I get upset when…

_____
_____
_____
_____
_____

★ List three ways you can calm yourself down.

_____
_____
_____
_____
_____

★ Name one person you can talk to when a situation makes you feel angry, sad, or frustrated.

★ Every day after school, rate your happiness level in a journal. Write down situations that happened at school and how you dealt with them. Be sure to include the ways you kept your calm during those situations.

★ Every night before you go to bed, write down three things you're most proud of yourself for accomplishing that day.

Break the Cycle

★ Do you notice that you say more hurtful things when you are in a bad mood?

★ Write down three things that put you in a bad mood. After identifying what situations lead you to saying hurtful things, try to be fully aware of when these situations occur.
 1.
 2.
 3.

★ Set three new goals for yourself to accomplish within the next month. Have these goals relate to school and friends.
 1.
 2.
 3.

★ Write down three people you feel you could apologize to for something you did or said that hurt their feelings.
 1.
 2.
 3.

★ Write a letter to these people in a journal you have at home. You don't have to send this letter. Write down what happened in your life before you bullied him or her.

★ Go up to these people over the next month and apologize for your actions.

Treat Others the Way You Want to Be Treated

★ Before you say something mean to someone, put yourself in their shoes. How would you feel if this were said to you?

★ Think of a time you were mistreated. Write down how you felt and what happened.

★ Now think of a time you helped someone and made him or her feel better. How did that make you feel?

★ How do you want others to treat you?

★ What does "treat others as you want to be treated" mean to you?

★ So do it!

Take a break, Super Girl!

Come back and pick this
up when you're able to.

You're doing GREAT!

CHAPTER
19

Bullying-Solution
Method for Option C

This chapter will help you figure out your action plan when you see your friend being bullied or bullying someone else. Answer these three questions to determine which Bullying-Solution Method Action Plan best works for you. We suggest you review all three methods so you can practice them all.

1. Are you comfortable speaking up when you see someone else being bullied?

2. Do you think it'd be better for an adult to stop the boy or girl from bullying someone?

3. If you weren't around the situation when it happened, would you still feel like doing something about it?

If you have more to say to question 1, your Bullying-Solution Method is Take a Stand.

If you have more to say to question 2, your Bullying-Solution Method is Get Your Back Up.

If you have more to say to question 3, your Bullying-Solution Method is After It Happens.

Take a Stand!

★ When you see another person being called names or being picked on, try to put yourself in their shoes to imagine how it might feel. Describe it here.

★ Depending on the situation, you may be able to tell the bully to stop the hurtful behavior. Have a statement ready to go. What is the statement you would say to that person? Be clear. Be loud. Write it out here.

★ Grab your friend who is being bullied and calmly walk away.

Get Your Back Up!

★ If you feel uncomfortable stepping in when you see a friend being bullied, or if the situation is dangerous, then let an adult know what is happening. If the first adult doesn't do anything about the problem, seek out another trusted adult to take action. Write down three adults at school you could tell and you KNOW would do something.

★ When you get home, tell your parent or guardian what happened, and ask him or her to call the principal.

★ Get to know your school counselor so you can tell this person when you witness a bullying situation happening at school.

★ If you feel too scared to say something, write a note without signing it. Turn in the note to the front office, but be sure to tell them you don't want your name in the report.

After It Happens

★ Ask your friend who was bullied how he or she is doing. It's always good for that person to know you are being supportive.

★ Ask him or her if they need anything.

★ Offer to walk with him or her to the school counselor's office.

★ Ask if he or she wants to sit with you at lunch.

★ Ask if your friend would mind if you told a teacher about what happened.

CHAPTER 20

Personal Promises

The last part of our workbook involves the Personal Promise. Cut out all of the Personal Promises in this workbook. These are here for you to make your own positive affirmations.

Create a Personal Promise around your home life, your school life, your family, and your friends.

Have fun and get creative! Write down a Personal Promise every day for one month, and be sure to DO that Personal Promise!

Great job, Super Girl!

Personal Promise

Personal Promise

Severson Sisters
Tips to Improve
Self-Esteem

Positive affirmations – Girls have a tendency to compare themselves to other girls, whether she's a peer or a celebrity. This is a slippery slope that can lead to unhealthy habits. Every time your daughter compares herself to another girl, have her write down and read out loud something positive she loves about herself and something positive she loves about her life. Make sure it's something different every time. Get her used to expanding her list of loves! Buy her a cute notebook that she can use for these exercises. Have fun with it, and make this a habit you and your daughter to do together.

Powerful and open communication – Talk, talk, talk. One great way to open dialogue is by creating a dream board together. Flip through magazines with your daughter and ask her to tear out images or words she's drawn to. It's a great conversation starter that will lead to what's she feeling about her current life. Use this as an opportunity to get to know her friends and the kind of influence they have on your daughter's life. Dream boards provide great inspiration for who we will become. Make this a monthly task and have fun with it. Let the conversation flow!

After-school activity – After-school activities provide a structure to life that keeps children engaged. Research shows that youth involved in academics, the arts, sports, or community activities are more likely to develop confidence and good self-esteem. Find a program that fits your daughter's interest and enroll her. And, as her interests change, her after-school activity should, too. She should always be engaged in something she's passionate about every school year.

Healthy habits – Encourage girls to love their bodies regardless of the shape, scale, or differences between them and their peers. Loving our bodies comes down to forming positive and healthy habits for the mind, body, and soul. Help her form a healthy relationship with food by teaching her how to make meals from ingredients bought at a local farmer's market. By helping her form a healthy relationship with food, she can avoid pitfalls with body-image issues as she continues to evolve. By fueling her body better, she'll feel better, which sparks great self-esteem.

Dedicate time to interests – Girls are busy! But whether it's a weekly or biweekly routine, encourage her to dedicate time to her personal interests that she can work on at home.

By creating something for herself, by herself, she has the opportunity to shine and display her individuality without worrying about peer influence that might stifle her sparkly self. Praise her for the effort she puts into bettering her life. Who knows, maybe this can be a fun project the entire household can get into! Pretty soon you'll have the next So You Think You Can Dance? team on your hands!

CHAPTER 22

How to Deal with a Bully

1. Nobody can take power away from you. You can handle anything. Repeat : "I can handle anything." "I'm beautiful, powerful and in charge of my life."

2. At Severson Sisters, we put emphasis on the importance of surrounding ourselves with positive, powerful peers. Create friends with these kids and stick with them. These kids are the ones who will help you stand up to the bully and help you avoid him or her until the situation is resolved. Sometimes you'll have to do this by joining a new group or organization, so ask your parents for help finding the right program for you.

3. The first thing you should do is tell the bully to stop. You must stand up for yourself. Say, "You know what, Carrie, don't do that. It's not cool."

4. Shrug off the comment as if it didn't mean anything. Walk away calmly as if you have all the confidence in the world and just had a great conversation with someone you really like. Avoid the bully; create a new route to your locker or next class. If you have time, go somewhere that you feel safe to regroup your thoughts.

5. Kids have to tell an adult they trust. You must be very specific about how a bully made you feel. Do you feel threatened, scared, or angry? These are important feelings to bring up to adults. Everyone needs to know about what's happening at school. It's the only way the bully's parents, guardians, and teachers are going to know to watch his or her behavior and address changes that have to happen.

CHAPTER
23

Bullying Resources

Stop Bullying

http://www.stopbullying.gov/

Pacer's National Bullying Prevention Center

http://www.pacer.org/bullying/?gclid=CLTSgOLkrKsCFQJUgwodKjr_2g

Teens Against Bullying

http://www.pacerteensagainstbullying.org/#/home

Stomp Out Bullying

stompoutbullying.org

Empowered Kidz

http://www.empoweredkidz.com/

Severson Sisters

http://www.seversonsisters.org/category/information/

The Severson Sisters Super Girl Guide To: Respect Team

Carrie Severson, Founder and CEO

Carrie Severson is our founder and CEO, and she loves her job! She knew, even as a little girl, that she was meant to make a difference in the world. That feeling of wanting to shine and lead was buried, though, because she was made fun of, left out, and bullied throughout her childhood, typically because she was heavier than other girls her age. She spent a lot of her childhood ashamed of her body, depressed, and worried that she would be embarrassed in front of her peers. Though she lacked self-esteem as a girl, she loved to dance and thrived on stage. She found that having a creative outlet gave her the freedom to be herself.

Carrie sought to create a program that bridges self-compassion and social behavior. The key that would bridge the two together would be creative objectives. She spent two years researching how creativity was related to self-esteem and how self-compassion played a role in youth development.

In January of 2011, she took a leap of faith and launched Severson Sisters. With the encouragement of her sister, Holly, and the rest of the Severson family, Carrie took off.

She believes her life's purpose is to be a light for any girl who needs it. Her motto and intention for her life is to continue to expand her light and the light of Severson Sisters.

Advisory Board

Holly Severson Hammerquist

Holly is an integral spoke in this wheel—and the real sister in Severson Sisters! As an educator in Phoenix, Holly brings so much of her education and experience to our programs. Holly makes sure that the girls enrolled in the Severson Sisters Super Girl Program always show their true colors. She strives to do her personal best every day and expects the same from her students and the people she surrounds herself with. She enjoys empowering girls. She is currently enrolled in a master's degree program, studying curriculum.

Larissa Rzemienski

Larissa is a licensed professional counselor and serves as an University of Phoenix Faculty at in the fields of psychology and human services. She has more than ten years of experience in the field of psychology, including working as a high school guidance and counseling chair, teen crisis hotline supervisor, and juvenile probation counselor. She received a bachelor of psychology degree and master of counseling psychology degree at Arizona State University. She aslo completed an M.B.A. in marketing management at University of Phoenix. Larissa has an eleven-year-old daughter. Having lost her husband just a few years ago, Larissa has a deep understanding of grief and loss issues from her own perspective as well as her daughter's.

Shirley Barna

Shirley has a passion for psychology and working with children. She has over ten years of experience working with children, families, and adults as a counselor, problem solver, and advocate. Shirley received a bachelor of science degree in psychology with a minor in family studies at Northern Arizona

University. At age 15, Shirley's passion for working with children began at her first job working at a summer camp with children with cerebral palsy, intellectual disabilities, and physical handicaps. She continued working with children in various capacities as a summer camp counselor, lifeguard, and swimming coach. After college, Shirley worked as a social worker for the state of Arizona and had the experience of working with hundreds of children and families. Shirley currently works in the field of human resources as a director of employee relations, where she is able to use her psychology degree by assisting nearly 1,000 employees with employment-related conflicts and problems. Although she is no longer working directly with children, Shirley continues to feed her passion by serving on boards of directors for nonprofit groups in Phoenix that raise money for various children's charities, and she also completed countless hours of organizing and participating in hands-on activities with girls and young women. Shirley believes that her passion for working with mental health issues and giving stem from caring for a father who has battled his own mental health illness for her entire life.

Laura Madden

Laura works as a holistic lifestyle coach, personal trainer, yoga instructor, and model. She completed a bachelor of science in kinesiology from the University of New Hampshire, and multiple certifications in health- and fitness-related studies thereafter. Originally from Boston, Laura resides in Scottsdale, Arizona, with her husband and two dogs, and is extremely passionate about inspiring people to live a healthful, holistic lifestyle, based on her life experience and many studies. She enjoys traveling, whole-food cooking, exercising, and entertaining friends, family, and her dogs.

Molly Minson

Molly is a speech therapist who received her degree from Arizona State University and works in the public school system. She is licensed by the Arizona Department of Health and the Arizona Department of Education. For several years, she has worked to meet the speech and language needs of special-education students from diverse backgrounds with varying disabilities. She enjoys laughing with her students every day and watching them grow. She grew up mainly in Arizona and had an active childhood filled with playing sports and being creative through art. Molly still enjoys creating art, whether she is developing therapy materials, painting glass, or crafting. She has always cared about helping others.

CHAPTER 25

Journal

Use these blank pages to keep a journal for the next 30 days!

_____

_____

_____

_____

_____

_____

_____

_____

_____

_____

_____

_____

_____

_____

_____

_____

_____

_____

_____

_____

_____

_____